Beyond Words: A Symphony of Passion and Action

by

Iris Sita McKee

Copyright 2024 Iris Sita McKee

ISBN: 978-1-917129-39-8

First published 2024

For Almighty God, my family and all my loved ones

Reviews

"I cannot recall ever seeing an inspirational book written by a nurse for nurses, and so I read this with a sense that the author spoke to 'me' and wrote from a shared lived experience, which was inspiring. Your caring and compassion come through strongly. Many will be helped by this"

-Heather Caudle (Chief Nursing Officer - NHS)

"Captivating, interesting, and reaffirms spirituality, which, in the writer's view, is an important aspect of her personal and professional life."

-Rev. Dr Josiah Anyinsah (Head of Pastoral and Spiritual Care - NHS)

"I liked your stories and how you used your experiences to change yourself, more than being told what you should do. I sincerely admire that you are writing and sharing with readers your passion, your faith and your wisdom."

-Denise Amoss (Managing Director - Quantum People)

"This book is a collection of ten letters/essays on the major life themes that can cause personalities to pause, become stunted or go adrift in their development as they pursue long term personal and career targets. While at one level almost autobiographical as the outworking of one woman's ongoing pilgrimage into the future, these reflections seek at the same time to provide helpful footholds up which readers can climb towards achieving their own cherished aims."

-Mark Rudall (Retired Priest)

"Easy to read, beautifully written and inspirational. I really liked the quotes at the beginning of each chapter and where relevant in other parts of the text and found these to be inspirational."

-Melanie Hobbs (International Recruitment and Retention Project Lead – NHS)

Contents

Preface

In life, we often find ourselves at a crossroads, grappling with decisions about our career paths. Some of us are in jobs that don't resonate with our aspirations, while others harbor dreams that seem distant, almost unattainable.

Whether you're a seasoned health or social care professional seeking change or a wide-eyed dreamer unsure of where to start, this book is crafted to inspire anyone, regardless of age or prior experience, in discovering their true calling. This book motivates and inspires readers who are navigating the road of career choices and aspirations.

Within these pages, you'll find some strategies, ideas, and some real-life experiences to help you navigate the maze of career choices and workplace challenges, and find direction. The author shares that spirituality and faith are significant to her personal and professional life. This may encourage those seeking to unearth their passions, define their goals, and take decisive steps toward a more meaningful professional life.

This book does not promise magic formulas, quick fixes, and it's definitely not a self-help book. Instead, it offers a roadmap, encouraging introspection and deliberate planning, and is meant to stimulate readers. It's a companion for those looking to shape their destiny whether they have a clear vision or are starting from a blank sheet.

May this book serve as a beacon of practical wisdom, igniting your drive and aiding you in forging a path that aligns with your ambitions. Embrace these pages as a resource to chart your course towards a career that resonates with your true aspirations and values.

A Tapestry of Beginnings: Weaving Your Career Story

"The key to success is to start before you're ready."
-Marie Forleo

Dear Reader,

Habakkuk 2:2-3 says, *"Then the lord replied: 'Write down the vision and make it plain on tablets so that a herald may run with it. For the vision awaits an appointed time; it speaks of the end and will not prove false. Though it lingers, wait for it; it will certainly come and will not delay."* Everyone has that dream to be something, or **"someone"** at some point. You must have thought to yourself at least once if what you were doing was what you wanted to do. Well, I'm also a person who resonates with this immensely. It all started many years ago when my desire to be the person I'd always wanted to be reached its peak, and it was also when I started having a family. I didn't want to do a job I'd hate for the rest of my life. I wanted something that would make me want to jump out of bed and the only thoughts running through my mind would be that I'd be making a difference in this world.

It wasn't easy of course; with the great decision came obstacles aplenty, and my life was far from what I thought an ideal candidate for the job I wished for would be. The people around me seemed to think the same; it was always "where would you get the time, your children need you, how will you manage both full-time studies and a young family, **Nursing** is a dying profession, no one values **Nurses**, it doesn't pay well," and so on. I wouldn't let these stop me from being and living the life I'd always wanted. At the time, I believed no choice was easy and that nothing good in life comes without challenges. Every choice for me seemed laborious; however, I realised I needed to choose my hard and then work for it, so I decided to work for it.

There is no right time to start; you can never be fully prepared before you take that leap of faith. As Marie Forleo once said, **The key to success is to start before you're ready**. And so, that is exactly what I did. After countless efforts at searching my soul for what it truly yearned for, I realised that what brought me true happiness was helping others and caring for them. It made my life more meaningful and brought value to this world. I loved to help solve their problems and empower them with the knowledge that they too can bring more value into their lives by actioning their goals. This was my passion; this was who I wanted to be. Let me walk you through my journey, step by step, breath by breath, so that you too can feel what I felt, and perhaps my message will reach out to you.

Every person is capable of bringing value to this world. Do not at any cost let anything stop you from being who you want to be.

I had done my research on everything I needed to start my journey as a full-fledged nurse. I started by looking into the qualifications needed to enroll in the Bachelor of Science in *Nursing* programme. Further, I had to decide on a specialisation, for which I chose mental health nursing, and considered factors like programme accreditation, curriculum, and clinical experiences. I then proceeded to apply for the course and began my nursing degree.

During the first year of my course I was walking around the campus and saw pictures of previous students who had won awards in their nursing specialty. I was simply amazed by them; it gave me that push I needed to excel in my field. I knew I wanted my face to be there too one day; I too wanted to be that person who gave someone else the hope to excel and succeed in their career.

Keeping this in mind, I received an award for excellence in practice when I completed my nursing degree. I couldn't have been happier. I knew that this was thanks to my vision, hard work, commitment, dedication, and mainly my desire to help others. I also completed the required coursework and clinical rotations. After successfully obtaining my nursing registration, I secured a job and took the initiative to enroll in continued education programmes focused on mental health nursing. I aimed to further develop my skills and expertise in the field, keeping myself updated and open to opportunities.

I'd also faced financial challenges down the road, but as the saying goes, *where there is a will there is a way*, and I managed to find a solution yet again. I'd researched and applied for scholarships and grants designed for students on my chosen professional course. There are countless options for financial aid, including student loans, grants, and work-study programmes. Working part-time while attending college also offsets educational expenses to some extent.

While faced with a lack of experience, take advantage of every opportunity you are given during your education to gain hands-on experience and build skills; no matter how big or small, take it. Volunteer work, internships, and externships are also excellent for gaining professionalism in your job, as well as to further hone your skills and practical experience.

The final task was to achieve work-life balance and dispel biases, and the first step to this was to learn the art of time management. It may seem challenging at first but experimenting with various strategies to manage your work, school, and personal life responsibilities will most definitely prove helpful. You will end up developing the perfect strategy that prioritises tasks concerning realistic goals and gives you a well-balanced schedule.

Remember this: it is of utmost importance to have a strong support system all through the journey. We tend to get too immersed in our work and achieving our goals. We sometimes don't think highly of maintaining relationships, but the role they play is crucial in ways you may not have imagined. Make sure to spare time for your family, friends, and loved ones as they will always hold your hand through a challenge and keep you from falling even when you lose faith in yourself. As humans we are social creatures that always crave love and understanding. It is as important as air to us.

Finally, we come to self-care and love which should be one of your top priorities as it is essential in maintaining physical and mental well-being. Make sure to exercise, ensure proper nutritional intake, and practice relaxation techniques. Dedicating time and attention to self-care serves as a powerful antidote to the stresses and demands that surround us. The practice of self-care lays the groundwork for a balanced and fulfilling life.

Keep improving your skills, knowledge, and competence while remaining dedicated and you've already dispelled all the biases. Hard work and consistency will make you invaluable. Reach out to experienced professionals and ask them to mentor you. This increases your prowess considerably. Not only are you being guided by the best, but your network is also growing. Keeping up to date with the latest certifications and courses also helps you stay efficient and evolving. Keep these tips in mind and you'll become a force to be reckoned with.

Challenges exist in every profession but with the right mindset, perseverance, dedication, and continuous learning, you're pretty much equipped with everything you need to walk over any obstacle that comes your way and succeed in your career.

"Create the highest, grandest vision possible for your life because you become what you believe."

-Oprah Winfrey

AI-generated picture

Multi-tasking: completing my coursework while bonding with my one-year-old son

The Resilient Mindset

"You may encounter many defeats but you must not be defeated."

-*Maya Angelou*

Dear Reader,

Oftentimes, I find solace in pondering upon one of my cherished Bible verses, ***Philippians 4:13***, which reassures me that I can accomplish anything with the strength bestowed upon me by Christ. From the moment I was qualified as a nurse there was a lot I wanted to do, and I was more than ready to start making a difference. I wasn't entirely perfect and still had a lot to learn, so I had to get my hands dirty and start from basics by working long hours. As a first-timer at a job, I started to truly learn and understand only when I ventured outside of my ***comfort zone,*** which was working '9 – 5' jobs in the community. The variable long shifts came with their physical and emotional challenges on myself and my young family, but I was determined not to be defeated at the first hurdle.

For example, three months into my career as a newly qualified nurse, I struggled to balance my responsibilities as a mum and a nurse. I was constantly worried when my childcare plans fell through which then impacted on my work commitments. I'd come home exhausted and unable to have meaningful interactions with my family. I had less post-qualification experience and there were fewer community nursing job opportunities for a newly qualified nurse that could meet my personal needs. At times, I felt I was failing as a mum as it appeared I was prioritising my career over my family.

I had to be bold to find balance, which meant seeking another job that offered a flexible work pattern. I didn't let my inadequate nursing experience hold me back at the interview. I demonstrated to the panel I'd be an asset to the hospital if hired. I got the job with the opportunity to choose my set 12-hour shifts, which were the same every week and brought balance, normality and stability to my personal and professional life. I was able to focus on the job and learn the skills I needed to become an outstanding competent and compassionate nurse.

Staying in your comfort zone might seem like a pleasant idea but it is nothing but a misconception. Everything you need to grow lies outside your comfort zone, so go ahead and challenge yourself to overcome the discomfort. This is how we develop a *growth mindset*. I quickly established relationships with my patients and clients, asked questions, and gained knowledge from experienced and novice staff. I also made some good friends with the team both clinical and non-clinical while learning from them simultaneously. I deeply yearned to have a positive effect on the lives of my patients and for that very reason I wanted to be the best at what I did. *Believe in yourself* and you can most definitely overcome any obstacle!

I took each *challenge* as a steppingstone instead. I set aside 30 minutes every day to think about the difficulties I encountered at work. Reflecting on the same with my coworkers, mentors, family, and on my own helped me to gain more perspective on issues. It also **expanded my network** in a way. People love to talk about themselves, and the best way to develop great connections is to talk about the things they're passionate about.

It was when I'd be on my way home that I'd have the most insight. I feel that's when I finally get a moment of peace from the day's events and see things clearly. I'd think of the why, what, how, and ways to improve on whatever I'd encountered that day. One of the biggest challenges I faced was when I was pursuing my master's degree while in a full-time nursing role and looking after my young family. I continued to give my all to get better at my job. I think that regardless of whether or not we're fast or slow learners, **consistency** is the key to success. Finding a reason to **drive** you makes a whole lot of difference. In my case, my desire to help others kept pushing me forward.

I was constantly bombarded with the question of what exactly my **goal/dream job** is in life from a very young age. Some people might've had it all figured out, but the majority of us have no clue of what we're doing. I feel that it's completely alright to be clueless and confused, so long as we keep trying, even if it is later on in life, it is never too late to work toward your goals. I embarked on my journey by setting forward **small achievable goals** at each stage of my nursing journey which then enabled me to apply for new nursing roles in line with my goals. I started as a staff nurse on a psychiatric inpatient unit and then applied for a role as a community psychiatric nurse to take care of and provide treatment for patients at home which would empower them to live independently.

Now there's this thing called *resilience*, but what exactly is it? Resilience is like a superhero power that enables us to conquer tough times and tricky situations. It's the ability to bend and flex our thoughts, feelings, and actions, so we can handle whatever the world throws at us, both from the outside and within ourselves. I challenged myself to apply for senior leadership roles even when I was doubtful of my abilities. I was faced with disappointments and closed doors from every angle. I'd then think of the reason why I started, keep moving, and find solutions. I overcame the doubts with support from my mentors who encouraged me to go for it and guided me.

Lastly, never forget to celebrate your *wins* regardless of how small or big they may be. My way of doing this was to do my signature little dance while singing praises to God. Throughout your journey of challenging yourself, take time to recognise and celebrate your accomplishments. Rewarding yourself makes a difference in both how you feel about yourself as well as how you are perceived. It is the best way to nourish your soul and body. You are your biggest asset, so treasure it!

I'd like you to look at your journey as a series of steppingstones to achieving your dream goals, starting from *finalising your goals* so you know exactly what it is you want, and *breaking them down* to clarify them. As we go further in life we are faced with various challenges on the road. This is where we develop a mindset of *growth and resilience* to smoothen the path and move forward. Don't hesitate to *reach out* to coworkers, mentors, family or people who value you when you need clearer insights or advice to improve.

Don't fall into the trap of a fixed mindset by ignoring constructive feedback from others, feeling threatened by the success of others, and hiding your flaws so that you don't feel judged by others. Instead, view feedback from others as a source of information and as an opportunity to learn. We should view the success of others as a source of inspiration and motivation to improve ourselves.

With each step, we get better, stronger, sharper, and wiser. Meet as many *professionals* as you can who already work at your dream job. They will know better as they have already walked down the same path and will give you a heads up on what to expect, saving both your energy and time. This will entail stepping out of your *comfort zone*, but it is not impossible. Envision yourself at your destination and keep marching forward. Finally, *embrace the feedback* you receive from colleagues, managers, and mentors and stay *up to date* with your intel. Use it to boost your performance and effectively move forward.

Remember that pushing yourself and conquering challenges is a process that takes time, discipline, perseverance, and a positive attitude. Maintain your focus on your goals, continue to learn, and adjust to changes along the road. I place heavy emphasis on the fact that there is no failure so long as you keep trying. The only obstacle that exists is you; only your expectations of yourself have been stopping you. Let go of that and you will see yourself soar. My dear reader, I wish you all the best. May you reach and conquer new horizons!

"It is not the mountain we conquer but ourselves."
-Edmund Hillary

AI-generated picture

Celebrate Wins: my way of celebrating little wins is dancing to my favourite gospel music

Navigating Different Perspectives

*"Go boldly and honestly through the world. Learn to love
the fact that there is nobody else quite like you."*

-Daniel Radcliffe

Dear Reader,

We all crave a sense of connection and belonging and thrive
on interactions with others, but this also creates room for a
lot of conflict. I was a person who tended to avoid conflict
as much as possible; however, through my work I realised
that I had to face them whether I liked them or not as they
played a crucial role in the flow of my work. All of us have
different values and aspirations in life and this may lead to
clashes with people we meet in various walks of life.

This is where *social* and *interpersonal* skills come into
play. I didn't learn these through my nursing degree but
more through my experiences with different personas I met
at work. At times it felt like no one understood me. All I
wanted to do was make a difference; however, everyone
else doesn't need to think the same way we do. These
experiences, as unpleasant as they were, shaped me a lot
both as a person and a professional. As much as experience
improves our social skills, making a conscious effort to
learn and practice effective communication skills will help
you excel enormously.

One challenging experience I encountered in my first
management role positively shaped my leadership skills, as

I chose to learn from the negative event. I felt some of my colleagues had already judged me before starting in post. I experienced a hostile reception from a colleague on my first day. That same day I made a management decision by prioritising the safety of patients in our care, but I was challenged by the colleague and I was reported to my line manager. I encountered daily challenges and felt my ability to problem-solve was being tested.

Being human, I found some days more frustrating than others and one day my emotions got the better of me. A meeting that was meant to support some colleagues to address problems turned sour. I felt I was being verbally attacked by my colleagues when a question I asked with genuine intention to address staff burnout was taken out of context. One colleague spoke to me harshly which surprised me, and I immediately found myself in a defensive mode justifying why I had been off sick. I was in an emotionally vulnerable state prior to the meeting as I had just returned from sick leave due to having a car accident and was feeling undervalued. My team had not shown any concern or compassion during my time off work.

The situation was distressing and I lost my composure. The objective of the meeting had changed to everyone complaining and no one listening. Some unkind words were directed at me, which was a wake-up call. I realised I was not dealing with the situation wisely. I took deep breaths and calmly brought the meeting to an end and walked away. On my way home after work, I reflected on the issue and my actions. I decided not to call meetings to discuss sensitive issues when I'm in an emotional state of mind; this ensured that I actively listened without taking it personal. I discussed the nursing and midwifery code of conduct with my colleagues during supervision and encouraged adherence to it to foster a respectful workplace. I carefully thought through and planned to address that particular conflict in a way that didn't make my colleagues feel I was blaming them. I apologised for not listening and said 'we' can both work on being professional rather than saying 'you' should work on being respectful.

During those times it was incredibly hard to keep my eyes ahead as I was constantly getting beaten down from various directions. I experienced brief periods of low mood, anxiety, and exhaustion. I was overwhelmed and unhappy. I had to dig deep to find meaning and motivation to keep moving forward. I took *support* from my loved ones – friends, family, and mentors – to stay true to myself. You understand the value of your loved ones when you go through the most difficult times of your life. The small chat I would have with them would instantly refresh and clear my mind, helping me to focus on what matters.

The *realisation* I achieved afterward was a beautiful moment of euphoria. I knew that I was unique in my way and that people did not have to understand my way of thinking. I had a goal to achieve and no one person or thing was going to stop me from getting there. I was the sole creator and achiever of my goal through Christ who strengthens me – to help others and make a difference. That sentence would instantly get me pumped up and get back to action. It's like that one sentence that holds a lot of meaning. Keep it close and you will be able to get out of the emotional block you find yourself in.

I felt that the best way to find encouragement was to give myself words of affirmation. I would tell myself that my heart and mind are clean, and as an honest person, I want to do good. I am courageous, confident, bold, brave, and fearless. I would also recite **Psalm 139:14**: "I praise you because I'm fearfully and wonderfully made; your works are wonderful; I know that full well." The affirmations worked like magic spells. The psychological impact affirmations have on the human brain is not to be underestimated. It may not seem like much but they can make a world of difference. These affirmations enabled me to stay strong to overcome the challenges I was experiencing. I encourage you to find your own powerful sentences or words that are personal to you, to use during difficult times.

I tapped into the *courage* that lay hidden in me and constructively challenged unkind decisions and actions from senior colleagues. However, the first time was scary as I wasn't sure how to be direct without coming across as confrontational toward my colleagues in senior roles in expressing my concerns. I knew my value and worth and wanted to work well with others to achieve our common goal of keeping patients and clients safe and well.

I thought from various *perspectives* to understand how each person would look at a given situation, put myself in the shoes of others, and broadened my horizons of thought. This helped me to objectively deal swiftly while conversing through conflict. I was able to put my view across in a *diplomatic* manner. It took me some time but it is most definitely an excellent skill to have. The boldness I found in myself was something that was not taught in my degree course, but rather life taught me and God blessed me with it as I desperately needed it to take the steps to achieve my next goals.

Now before you set forth on your journey of dealing with various egos, here are a few things to keep in mind. Firstly, manage your own emotions and reactions before responding to someone else, and practice developing a sense of *self-awareness*. This can help you build better relationships and find common ground. Do not let your emotions cloud your judgment; focus on using logic as a key factor here. Secondly, be *empathetic* and *listen* to what people have to say. When I say listening to what people say can completely change the outcome of a situation, I mean it. By listening to them you are showing that their words matter and that they are of significance in the situation concerned. People love to be valued; this will give you a stronghold while dealing with them.

Thirdly, state your thoughts and ideas in a simple, clear, and concise manner. Get to the point, but avoid being confrontational, as this can make the opposing party seem at fault and hence escalate conflicts. *Effective communication* is important while making your stance and getting a point across. Fourthly, find *common goals* while simultaneously *seeking feedback* and *assistance* if necessary. When both parties are concentrated on a single goal, you are bound to find ways to cooperate and concentrate your shared effort. This can promote collaboration and reduce conflicts caused by personal agendas.

Encourage *open* and *constructive* feedback from your peers, including those with challenging personalities. Feedback can help address any misunderstandings and improve your overall relationships. It also helps us to improve our ways and get better at what we do. In case you find it challenging to deal with a particular person, seek guidance from a trusted colleague, mentor, or supervisor who can provide advice or mediate the situation. Do not hesitate to reach out for help when the situation requires it. Try to resolve it on your own first; if you see that it isn't faring well, go ahead and seek advice from someone experienced at the same.

Lastly, make sure to *set solid boundaries* while dealing with people. Occasionally you will bump into that personality who will most definitely test your limits and try to make your everyday life a little harder, day after day. I'm sure you've heard of the term *toxic* people; when someone's ego consistently negatively impacts your work or creates a toxic environment, it may be necessary to establish and enforce certain boundaries. Stand up for yourself respectfully and assertively as and when it is required. These points are not just going to help you in your work life; you will begin to see a change in all of your relationships when you practice these mindfully and consistently. Dealing with different egos at the workplace is a skill that can be developed over time. By practicing self-awareness, empathy, and effective communication, you can build better professional relationships and navigate workplace dynamics more effectively.

"You can do anything you want, even if you are being told negative things. Stay strong and find motivation."

-Misty Copeland

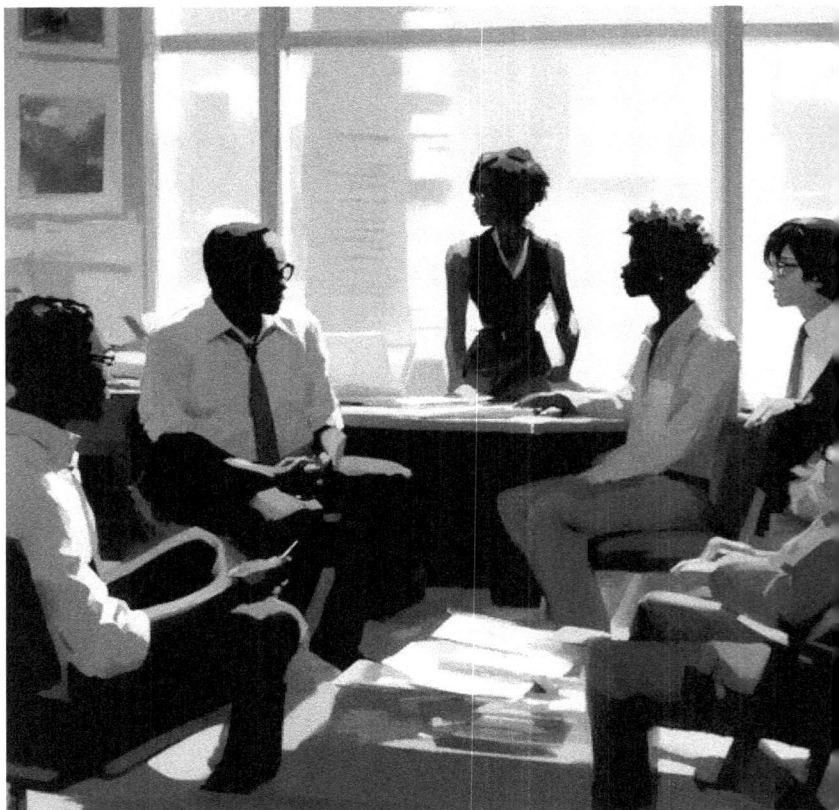

AI-generated picture

Diplomatic Conversations: I adopt a tactful approach when addressing workplace conflicts

Valuable Contributions, Unrecognised Efforts: The Helper's Dilemma

"No matter who you are, no matter what you did, no matter where you've come from, you can always become a better version of yourself."

-Madonna

Dear Reader,

Romans 13:8 says, *"Owe no one anything except to love one another, for he who loves another has fulfilled the law."* I often noticed that colleagues at work who were on a lower grade pay were less valued than others, in my experience. Showing genuine love and care by giving them the value they deserve has been very fulfilling and rewarding as they have risen to support me too in my time of need. This was when even the people in leadership positions, whom I had expected to help me, had no intentions of doing the same. Life is such that the most unexpected people come to your aid when you least expect it. After all, everything comes back to you in the end.

I remember a time when my steady act of care and compassion bore fruit. Most mornings as I walked into my office at work, I'd greet the cleaner and spend about five minutes chatting to them, in order to get to know them. I was being my authentic self and showed sincere interest in a colleague whom other clinical staff would ignore unless there was a need to speak to them. I was able to identify times they were experiencing work or personal life challenges and needed protected time to chat; I'd offer words of encouragement to reassure them. Little did I know my support was highly appreciated by this colleague.

There was a time when I had less than two hours to receive a hospital inspector. Everything appeared to be working against me that particular day. Staff called in sick, I had to multi-task, I worked in my role as manager and undertook clinical duties to minimise service disruptions. My cleaner colleague came to my rescue on the day and prioritised getting the meeting room ready so that I could host the inspector. They ensured wall posters were in place and other rooms and communal areas were all tidy and clean. Some of the tasks carried out by this colleague were not in their daily job description, such as running errands for me. I received positive feedback after the inspection which boosted my confidence as a manager and a leader. I later thanked and praised my colleague for going the extra mile to support me.

It is important to love and value people regardless of race, gender, religion, or background. Everyone deserves to be valued and appreciated. I encourage you to start valuing your friends, family, and work colleagues, and start spreading genuine love, care, and support without any ulterior motive. Be true to yourself and others. You never know how much your actions or words might mean to someone. We never know what one could be going through, so always be loving to those around you regardless of who they are.

Over my years in the career, I've made note of some important points that can help you in your endeavor of helping your colleagues as well as yourself. When you help those around you, you are automatically raising yourself too, and faster than you would if you focused solely on yourself. Everyone deserves to be seen and heard, so be the person who lifts others as you go. Here's how you can use them in your personal and professional life.

Be *empathetic* to your colleagues – listen, understand their concerns and feelings, and let them know you care for them and are genuinely there to support them. Everyone wants to be heard and understood. There is nothing more powerful and deep than simply listening to what one has to say. We all feel undervalued at some point in our lives. Let others know that it is normal to feel this way and that they are not alone in this walk of life. *Recognise* and *assure* them that their emotions are valid and their efforts are always significant.

Appreciate them for their work; no job is smaller than another. Nurture a positive team environment by giving *clear recognition* as and when necessary. Look for chances to acknowledge and praise both big and small contributions, just like you would cheer for a teammate in a game. Share these moments in team meetings or other platforms, and let them know that their achievements matter. Give sincere feedback for their hard work, skills, and successes. Imagine the workplace as a stage where each team member gets their moment in the spotlight. This practice not only boosts spirit but also builds *confidence*.

Introduce a culture of ***open communication*** within your team by establishing a safe space for colleagues to freely voice their concerns, free from the worry of judgment or negative consequences. Motivate them to contribute their thoughts, perspectives, and difficulties, nurturing an atmosphere of collaborative interaction. Emphasise the value of ***transparent communication*** – it's not just about speaking up but also actively listening. Think of your team as a place free of all judgment where everyone is not only welcomed but valued. By creating this kind of environment, we promote teamwork and ensure that each member feels heard and understood, hence fostering a workplace where open communication is not just a policy but a shared principle.

Step into the role of a ***mentor*** or facilitator to provide guidance, advice, and support to your colleagues when they seek it. Actively promote such events by either organising structured mentorship programs or encouraging informal mentoring relationships within the workplace. These interactions serve as valuable opportunities for individuals to not only build confidence but also gain insights from more experienced colleagues. By taking on this role, you contribute to a culture of ***continuous learning*** and ***professional growth***, fostering a collaborative environment where the wisdom is shared with those who are eager to learn.

Sometimes colleagues who are at lower tiers may not have access to the skills and resources that would help them enhance their skills; we've all been there, haven't we?

Guide them toward *workshops, courses,* or *conferences* that align with their goals. By supporting these initiatives, you actively contribute to their skill enhancement, knowledge, and overall personal development. Help them gain access to what it is they seek, and explore growth opportunities within the organisation, reinforcing the idea that their development is not just a personal goal but a part of the collective success of the team.

Lastly, there is nothing more important than your state of mind and health. Remind your colleagues of the importance of *self-care* and maintaining a *healthy work–life balance*. Help them explore strategies to manage stress, establish boundaries, and prioritise their well-being. If we are not well, there is only so much value one can provide, for one cannot pour from an empty cup. As much as work is important, other aspects of your life need to be tended to as well. Family, friendships, and relationships are all equally important, so make sure you aren't expending all of your energy just on work.

The previous point ultimately allows us to be the *supportive presence* that anyone can approach for guidance and encouragement as and when required. When we look after and spend an ample amount of time with ourselves, we can be there for the people around us. Offering our time and support to others when they need us can make a significant difference in them feeling valued and appreciated. Being consistent with care and understanding plays a big role in helping others not only feel better but also makes us a *reliable* entity.

Keep in mind that every individual deserves to feel appreciated and upheld in their professional setting. Follow these points and you can actively contribute to the establishment of a more inclusive and optimistic workplace for your colleagues. Cultivate a culture where each team member is not just acknowledged but genuinely respected and valued. These efforts work toward shaping an environment where everyone feels included and their contributions are recognised and appreciated. Help others by showing love and care regardless of their virtue, be human, and be kind.

"We can change the world and make it a better place. It is in our hands to make a difference."

-Nelson Mandela

AI-generated picture

Valuing Colleagues: I dedicate time to support my colleagues who need a safe space to talk

Guiding Lights: Trust Through Challenges

"Love and compassion are necessities, not luxuries. Without them, humanity cannot survive."

-Dalai Lama

Dear Reader,

Ephesians 4:31-32 says, *"Get rid of all bitterness, rage and anger, brawling and slander, along with every form of malice. Be kind and compassionate to one another, just as in Christ God forgave you."* **Trust** and **compassion** go far in various walks of life. Over the years, in my experience at work, I've seen them bring about miracles. One instance was when I realised that when my work environment fostered trust and compassion, I worked effectively with my colleagues, shared ideas, and asked for help regarding the issue at hand. This helped me do my job better, learn effectively, find joy at work, and also feel better.

On the other hand, when I worked at places that encouraged gossip, envy, and a culture of slander, the opposite happened. Your environment plays a crucial role in how well you perform overall. Suppose you were an extremely dedicated, honest, and goal-oriented worker in a lazy, unmotivated, and negative workspace. Naturally, you would see yourself mirroring these habits in no time. Humans tend to *adapt* and *copy* others to survive, which is why we are often advised to spend time around those who are where we aspire to be in life. A *healthy environment* helps to foster better talent, effective work, and a healthy mindset, of which trust and compassion are cornerstones.

Being part of a workplace that prioritised trust and compassion quickly impacted my professional well-being. Working in a place where colleagues trusted one another and embraced a culture of *kindness* not only heightened my job satisfaction but also elevated my morale. It was almost as if the atmosphere facilitated connection and collaboration. I felt like my contributions were recognised and valued, making my routine tasks meaningful and purposeful. There was a sense of *community* through trust and compassion which created a fulfilling work-life balance, making each day something to look forward to. It was something that I'd wake up to every day and feel exhilarated, not stressed.

While trust and compassion are not easy to find, I'd say you have *faith* in God and he shall guide you toward what you seek. This is in consideration that you too are making an effort to achieve your purpose. To be surrounded by people who you can trust and be compassionate with is also a blessing. They allow you to feel rooted, safe, and secure. Not only are you making others feel valued but you too are bound to get the benefits of *wisdom* from others who have walked your path. Listen carefully to those words and take your next step with consideration. Try not to act with haste.

An *open* and *honest* culture makes one feel safe and encourages better communication. When we know that we aren't going to be judged regardless of whether we are right or wrong, we bring out true, authentic ideas. Communication is boundaryless and free, allowing a vibrant exchange of thoughts and perspectives. I found myself being able to be my truest and most authentic self and enjoy the process as a whole! The absence of *judgment* fosters a collaborative spirit where diverse viewpoints are not only acknowledged but accepted. This openness not only improves the quality of communication but also establishes a foundation for trust amongst team members, creating a positive impact on the organisation as a whole.

Trust and compassion make me *feel valued* among my colleagues. I feel honored when they come to me for advice regarding their issues. It gives me a sense of *fulfillment* to see that I've created a space for them to feel heard and understood, just as they too have done for me. At times, one may seem rude or unpleasant; try to be kind and compassionate at such times, for you never know what they might be going through. Keep in mind, however, to ensure you've kept strong boundaries for yourself when you're out there and helping others. Never go beyond your means for the sake of helping others. It can be exhausting to keep being kind if people are taking advantage and draining you with excessive or unreasonable demands.

Another thing I'd like to stress upon would be the lack of, or perhaps *no stress*, even when you are in such an environment. Having a trustworthy bunch surrounding you takes off the extra load of thinking and carefully crafting what you say to others. I found myself far less stressed and burnout became a thing of the past when I was in a trusting and compassionate environment. It wasn't just about not feeling stressed; it was about having real support and understanding from my team. Knowing I could **depend** on my coworkers took away a lot of pressure. I could concentrate more on my work instead of being stressed about how I interacted with others.

It came to my attention that my team provided excellent service when we were trusting of each other. We were more inclined to get the job done as well as help each other in getting our tasks done. There was no *'I'* here; we functioned as a 'we.' I'd encourage using the word *'we'* when you work in a team as this gives a sense of collectedness and belonging. When people are focused on collectively getting a task done it is completed far more efficiently and effectively than when there is no cooperation and trust amongst fellow members. It's not just about completing tasks; it's about achieving shared goals and celebrating successes together. This **collaborative mindset** not only enhances the productivity of the team but also creates a positive and supportive work culture where everyone feels **valued** and **connected**.

I realised that fostering trust and compassion in the workplace cultivates a **positive** and **supportive** environment, leading to increased teamwork, satisfaction, loyalty, and productivity. This combination forms the backbone of a workplace culture where individuals want to contribute to betterment and work with passion. Making everyone feel included at work helps them work together smoothly, breaking down barriers and creating a strong sense of togetherness. When there's trust, people are more likely to openly share ideas, use their strengths, and team up on shared goals. This not only makes teamwork better but also makes people happier at their jobs because they feel valued and part of something important.

Lastly, I'd like to talk about loyalty. Loyalty grows because people see that colleagues and bosses genuinely care and **support** each other. When trust and compassion go both ways, it creates a place where everyone is committed to the organisation's goals. This boosts job happiness and loyalty, which in turn makes everyone work better. When everyone is valued and taken care of, **productivity** knows no bounds. Now, besides what others do and practice, always remember, be there for the ones who need you regardless of who they are, because kindness is unconditional, and a helping hand can make a world of difference.

"If you work really hard and you're KIND, amazing things will happen."

-*Conan O'Brien*

AI-generated picture

True Compassion: when my team genuinely care for each other through thick and thin

The Compassionate Leader

"The nature of humility, its essence, is to feel another's pain as one's own, and to act to take that pain away. There is nobility in compassion, a beauty in empathy, a grace in forgiveness."

-John Connolly

Dear Reader,

Matthew 14:14 says, *"When Jesus landed and saw a large crowd, he had compassion on them and healed their sick."* At some point in our work careers, we will be given the **responsibility** of being a leader, and this is a blessed opportunity to learn not only more about the various facets of people and time management but also how everyone does things in their unique ways. Now, this uniqueness of getting work done can be both a blessing and a curse, but it all comes down to how you deal with it. I'm sure you must have stumbled upon the word "compassion" now and then. Now, this word is key to becoming a wonderful leader. Becoming a *compassionate* leader involves developing empathy, understanding, and genuine care for people, especially your team members.

Compassion involves showing kindness, empathy, and understanding toward others, particularly in times of difficulty or pain. That innate urge to help someone when they're in need, especially when their pain echoes yours, would be an accurate description of exactly what compassion feels like to me, considering you do everything in your capacity to help them out. You must be wondering how being compassionate is going to alleviate your role as a leader. It makes you a better leader because it fosters trust, motivates your team, and helps resolve conflicts more effectively, creating a positive and successful work environment.

In the leadership roles I've held, I would make an effort to **actively listen** to my colleagues, and be **empathetic** by noticing their tiredness and encouraging them to take a day or two leave days when they are exhausted or showing some signs of early burnout. I'd suggest leave, if it is within my control to actively support them to address their challenges. If the cause of their stress or burnout was not within my influence to address, the suggested time off will provide them space to assess the cause and they are reassured of my support if and when needed. This not only benefits them but also the work they do, as people tend to perform better when they are in good shape both mentally and physically. I would also get involved in mundane tasks to alleviate pressure on the team. I'd do everything to be as understanding and helpful as possible. This is not an easy task but I know that my efforts are worth it when I see my team members working well with each other and putting in genuine efforts to get the task at hand done.

However, as I mentioned before, it is not always easy to be a compassionate leader, especially when challenges arise and I face resistance. Often these things are easier said than done, but me being me, I've always looked for solutions. It was in those times I dug deep and found the strength to overcome challenges by being *forgiving* and *empathising* with people and their struggles. Just like you, everyone has their struggles and day-to-day challenges to deal with besides their work. As challenging as it might be to understand every one of their situations, try putting yourself in their shoes and you will find yourself empathising much easier.

There were times when *stressful* moments had caused me to act out of character. I said things I didn't mean. It is difficult to maintain your cool when you might be going through a hard time yourself. You might feel like it's unfair on yourself, but trust me, we've all been there at least once. One of the aspects of being a leader includes exactly this, to keep a *clear* and level head when you deal with different personalities and difficult circumstances. Suppose you do happen to lose your cool and say something that may be perceived as disrespectful; reflect on it, and apologise to the individual involved. This not only shows humility in clearing the air but also ensures peace is rebuilt in the team by being kind.

I also made sure to *recognise* and *appreciate* my team whenever possible. This allows each individual to know that their contributions and efforts matter and are appreciated. This also motivates them to perform better and give it their very best. No one likes to work somewhere they feel undervalued and underappreciated for their hard work. By taking the time to recognise each of my team members' efforts, I made sure that the environment was positively inclined toward their professional well-being. I aimed to cultivate a workplace where everyone felt heard, respected, and motivated to contribute their best to our collective success.

Remember, *collective success* is more powerful than individual success when you work as a team.

Provide *emotional support* to your team whenever needed. Sometimes workloads are heavy and deadlines can be very stressful. At these times, it is essential to maintain calm and clarity to allow yourself as well as others to function properly. Having a level head also enables you to offer emotional support to those who require it. As a leader, you can also mentor your fellow peers. This not only allows you to clarify the concepts you've learned but also helps to promote their professional development.

Mentoring is an excellent means to cultivate a collaborative learning environment where everyone learns something from each other. Try taking a holistic approach to this and include other aspects of professional and personal development rather than focusing purely on work-related matters. This provides individuals with both personal as well as professional development.

Lastly, I learned to be *generous* with my time and knowledge in *assisting* my colleagues who needed support despite the discouraging challenges I encountered. Even as things were rough, I still made it a priority to be there for those who needed help. It took me a lot of effort, patience, and persistence to develop this skill, but over the years I've been able to get a hang of it, and I know that you can too. Persistence is key to mastering a skill; persistence and patience go hand in hand, I'd say. Helping others also boosted my mood and energy, as it is the one thing that has been and will always be uplifting to me. This generosity with time and knowledge is not just about problem-solving but also about instilling a sense of confidence and resilience in the face of challenges.

Compassionate leadership has significant benefits for both the individuals being led and the organisation as a whole. It fosters a sense of positivity and a supportive workplace culture, leading to increased employee engagement, satisfaction, and productivity. When team members help each other out, it creates a positive vibe in the workplace. This energy tends to spread, and people are more likely to help each other in return. It's like a chain reaction of good vibes that makes the whole work environment better. We're able to cultivate an environment of increased employee satisfaction by encouraging compassionate leadership, hence increasing productivity and positivity amongst everyone. Create an atmosphere you would like to work in, a place that you would want to come to every day, and put in your best efforts.

"A hero is an ordinary individual who finds the strength to persevere and endure in spite of overwhelming obstacles."

-Christopher Reeve

AI-generated picture

True Empathy: being mentally, emotionally and/or physically present to support your colleagues

The Nurse Entrepreneur

"Do what you were born to do. You just have to trust yourself."

-Beyonce Knowles

Dear Reader,

1 Peter 4:10 says, *"Each of you should use whatever gift you have received to serve others, as faithful stewards of God's grace in its various forms."* Even though it took me a long time to discover what my talent was, I'm glad I was patient with myself and life; the wait was worth it. I realised I had a spirit that naturally empowered, encouraged, educated, and enabled ***wellness*** in others. I firmly believe that nurturing every aspect of one's being could yield enduring benefits, fostering a future where investing in ***health*** and ***lifestyle*** is a priority. I knew it was my calling to help and bring others to their full potential. You know it's yours when it simply *feels* right. We all have that one thing that never tires us out and that we have an endless amount of energy for; you just never get tired of it!

I was always passionate about the ***wellness*** profession and serving others to embrace wellness within them. I believed that I could have a more significant impact on people's lives by expanding their focus beyond just nursing and providing services that would promote their overall well-being. I wanted others to have a well-rounded experience with me that goes to show them how they can become the best versions of themselves in the process. The ***holistic*** *development* of an individual can go a long way in the long run. Investing in your health and lifestyle is perhaps the best thing you can do for yourself and I wanted to help people do exactly that.

My talent is both a gift and a blessing, I feel. I desired greater autonomy to become a *wellness entrepreneur* and have the freedom to develop and implement God-given ideas and strategies to make a difference. I wanted to help others through all that I'd learned on my journey, make their paths easier, and help them become better versions of themselves in the process. This was the one thing that had always resonated greatly with me and gave me a sense of contentment and fulfillment. I diligently improved my skills, exploring holistic health, mental strength, and spiritual well-being deeply. Each day was a chance for me to connect wisdom with modern approaches, helping me form and understand inventive strategies rooted in *human wellness*.

As a *wellness entrepreneur*, I got to develop innovative and creative solutions to the problems I identified, and through continuous trial and error as well as deliberation, I was able to develop proper *solutions* to various issues. Being a wellness entrepreneur and doing what I was born to do gave me an immense sense of *personal fulfillment*. Although I'd discovered it much later in life, I was still happy that I had given it a shot and never gave up on my dreams. The late start didn't deter my spirit; instead, it instilled in me a profound belief that it's never too late to follow your passion. It was a reminder that determination knows no age limit. Each step I took and each idea I explored made me understand that persistence and dedication paved the way to success, regardless of everything else.

Another thing to keep in mind when you are an **entrepreneur** is to have a **strong vision** of what exactly it is that you want. When you have a defined end goal to achieve it is easier to persist even through tough times and challenges. It also makes the challenges and obstacles you face worth your time and effort. Moreover, a clear vision doesn't just help you to stay focused but also sparks strong passion and excitement. It gives a clear sense of purpose that goes beyond the current challenges, keeping the entrepreneurial drive alive. Every journey has its ups and downs, so be prepared mentally and have a positive mindset before you start on your journey.

One needs to be **organised,** to **plan,** and to have some **financial stability** to be able to get through the initial stages of the business – this can be quite challenging. This is most definitely not for the faint-hearted. Be strong and believe in God's sustaining power and also in the gifts you've been blessed with. Having faith that God will hold you and get you through anything acts as a support during tough moments. It gives comfort and confidence to handle uncertainties. This faith is like a guiding light, giving you hope even in the darkest times. At the same time, recognising and accepting the special abilities each person has is crucial.

Everyone has their ***unique talents*** that are special and unlike anyone else's. These talents, when understood and developed, help overcome obstacles. They form the basis for dealing with challenges encountered while starting a business. Also, have trust in your fellow workers that they will get the task at hand done with their unique talents too, and help and assist them when necessary. Building a ***strong belief*** in your abilities isn't just about being confident; it's about understanding the responsibility that comes with these special gifts. It's about using these talents to do good and make a positive impact while facing challenges. However, once you've started and you're well on the road, things become a little easier to handle and more stable. So, make sure you put in all good planning and effort when you start, and build a strong, unshakeable base.

I've mentioned before that I was a person who wasn't exactly a fan of taking ***risks*** in general, but I had to step out of my ***comfort zone*** and be willing to take risks, be unwavering in my faith, and be personally ready by continuously developing my skills and talent. But risks are an unavoidable part of starting as an entrepreneur, so start little by little, get yourself used to taking small risks and you'll get the hang of it for sure. I, too, started small, taking cautious steps toward my ***entrepreneurial*** journey. Initially daunting, these small risks eventually grew familiar to me. Over time, I became more adept at managing and even embracing risks. I soon realised that they were essential to entrepreneurial growth, both personally and as a whole.

My transition from risk-averse to risk-embracing wasn't instantaneous. It involved **consistent effort** and a willingness to step into discomfort. By starting small and gradually exposing myself to risks, I cultivated a mindset that can tackle challenges and work well amidst uncertainties. *Entrepreneurship* taught me that risk-taking is not about recklessness but about calculated steps toward growth. I encourage aspiring entrepreneurs to stay steadfast in their pursuits, remain patient, and stay dedicated to their vision. Growth never happens in a day; it takes time and consistent effort, so stay patient, dedicated, and focused on achieving your goals and you will most definitely get there.

"Dreams become reality when we put our minds to it."

-Queen Latifah

AI-generated picture

Boldness at Work: stepping out of my comfort zone to address a room full of experts

Embrace Challenges, Achieve Greatness

"Our greatest weakness lies in giving up. The most certain way to succeed is always to try just one more time."

-*Thomas A. Edison*

Dear Reader,

John 16:33 says, *"I have told you these things, so that in me you may have peace. In this world you will have trouble. But take heart! I have overcome the world."* I've been through a fair number of ***challenges*** in my personal and professional life. However, what truly amazes me is how some friends, family, and colleagues sometimes doubt that I've been through thick and thin to great extents. I guess maybe I don't seem like a person who's been through and seen a lot, but the challenges I've faced had both a ***mental*** and ***physical*** toll on me. Regardless, I've always tried to learn from those challenges, find strength and answers through them, and move on with my life. My challenges have only ever done me good, and despite the falls, I've always gotten back up, but much wiser and tougher.

One such difficult time was in my early teenage years when I had an opportunity to live away from home in a different country, in a Caucasian neighbourhood with a family friend, in order to experience western education. It was during this period I encountered racism for the first time. Some classmates spat on me and none were willing to partner with me in my physical education class during activities. I felt unhappy and isolated but I didn't give up and found a way to cope. The teachers became my friends and I learnt a lot from them. This gave me hope to carry on attending the school.

Fast forward a few years after, in my first job as a retail customer service assistant, I had another experience where work colleagues avoided sitting next to me on a bench if that was the only seat available in the staff cafeteria. Some customers wouldn't hand their money to me directly; they would leave it on the tills after I'd processed their purchases. I was upset during these times as it knocked my confidence and I felt I was a failure when I couldn't progress in that job. I decided to quit the job and find one that would value me as a person, as I couldn't see career development in that environment. I was able to move forward in life to succeed when I made a decision to forgive those people and chose not to be a victim. I've turned my negative experiences into strengths to encourage and support others who are going through similar situations, and I tactfully educate the bullies involved where I'm able to.

I've always seen **setbacks** and **failures** as opportunities for growth, hence I cultivated a positive mindset that allowed me to bounce right back from **difficult situations**. You might feel like everything is falling apart and nothing makes sense, but trust me, stay patient and you'll see why life put you through these trials. Believe that everything is happening for you and not to you. At times it takes a great failure to help you learn exactly what it is that you need to achieve your goals. Remain **patient** and you'll see the answers in the failures. It is failures that make you **stronger** and *wiser*. Don't fear failure; embrace it, and you will learn much more than you can imagine. Failure is a far more powerful teacher than success. Keeping a *positive mindset* through it all requires continuous training of the mind and persistence. Keep practicing and you'll most definitely get there.

Success does not come overnight. Setbacks are normal and I've learned to prepare for unexpected scenarios along the way. Life is all about the *unexpected*. Sometimes we find ourselves worrying far too much about the things we can't control. Learn to let these go, and try to do something about the things we can control. Success never goes in a straight line. There will be ups and downs, but don't falter; keep *persisting*, and lean on your loved ones for support when you need to. It may not seem clear right away, but every step, each effort you put into your goals, is truly going to be worth it. Seek out *advice* from a trusted source when you're confused, and don't hesitate to reach out to others more experienced than you, for they have walked the same path and know better how to tackle the adversities that follow.

I surrounded myself with a *supportive network* of mentors, peers, and fellow entrepreneurs who offered guidance and encouragement during difficult times. *Collaborative relationships* provided me with valuable insights, advice, and motivation. Having people who know their way around the career can be greatly helpful. You're able to learn more effectively and save time trying to figure out things on your own. You are also twice as motivated when you work with people who have the same end goal in mind as you. This is the essence of collaborative relationships; when more people focus their energy on achieving a ***single goal***, the goal is achieved much faster than it would be if approached single-handedly. Together, we moved faster toward success by pooling our energy and expertise toward shared objectives.

As I'd mentioned before, ***failure*** does not mean it's all over; it's a valuable learning experience. Every time things don't work out as planned, it doesn't mean it's the end of the road. Failure is more like a ***teacher*** than a roadblock. It's where we often learn the most. Instead of seeing it as a dead-end, I see it as a lesson. It helps me figure out what doesn't work and nudges me to find a better way. Being ***flexible*** can help you navigate challenges and seize new opportunities. With practice, you can build ***resistance*** to difficult scenarios and learn how to cope with the emotions that come with it. I made it my goal to become a flexible person when it comes to challenges, and the best way to build that flexibility is to put yourself into such situations again and again until you find yourself easily maneuvering your way through. When you become flexible you can handle a large diversity of tasks and situations with ease.

I ensure to practice ***self-care***, engage in activities I enjoy, and take breaks when needed. Maintaining a healthy mindset and energy level helps me confront challenges with resilience. Taking care of yourself is the single most important part of becoming the best version of yourself, and this in turn leads to you performing your best. It's kind of like the ***domino effect***. Investing in your health and well-being is the best gift you can give yourself. By prioritising self-care, I not only recharge my batteries but also enhance my *focus* and *creativity*. It's incredible how a well-rested mind can approach ***problem-solving*** with renewed vigor and clarity. Additionally, setting ***boundaries*** and knowing when to step back allows me to maintain a sustainable pace in both my work and personal life, ensuring long-term success and fulfillment.

I reflect and revisit my ***initial motivations*** and the passion that drove me to become an ***entrepreneur*** to keep my motivation intact and burning. Every time I find myself tired of the journey or doubtful, I remind myself of why I chose this path and how I started, especially how I've gotten this far. This boosts my motivation and I get up again to finish what I started.

Moreover, I find that taking time for ***introspection*** and ***self-assessment*** aids in refining my strategies and aligning them with my long-term goals. Occasionally, I seek feedback from mentors or trusted peers, valuing their insights in evaluating my progress and potential areas for improvement.

Continuous learning and ***self-development*** equip me with the knowledge and skills necessary to navigate challenges effectively. There is never an end to learning; there is always so much more that is yet to be discovered and ventured into. Each subject is vast like the sea; there is always room for more. Keep equipping yourself with the latest ***skills*** and ***knowledge*** to stay on track and ahead of the competition. Learning isn't just about gathering information; it's about using that knowledge to solve problems. It's like adding tools to a toolbox that I can use to overcome challenges. Learning isn't only for business; it helps me grow as a person too. I learn not just from books but also from people – mentors, experts, and other entrepreneurs.

Being *open* to new ideas and willing to *change* is important too. Learning involves not just gaining new knowledge but also unlearning old ideas that might not be helpful anymore. Every obstacle is a chance to learn and improve. Embracing the *unknown* and diverse perspectives fosters innovation, driving progress not only in business but also in personal development. Learning also ensures that your mind is always fresh and creative. *Learning* is the best medicine for stagnancy; to have an open mind you must always keep your mind awake and running. Overall, the journey of learning isn't just about being competitive – it's about growing personally, being adaptable, and becoming stronger.

"Do the best you can until you know better. Then when you know better, do better."

-Maya Angelou

"It always seems impossible until it's done."

-Nelson Mandela

AI-generated picture

No Mountain Too High: I see mountains in my life as my next success story

Words to Keep You Going

"Optimism is the Faith that leads to achievement."

-Helen Keller

Dear Reader,

Joshua 1:9 says, *"Have I not commanded you? Be strong and courageous. Do not be frightened, and do not be dismayed, for the LORD your God is with you wherever you go."* There are often times when we are consumed by fear and anxiety, but remember, there is no use worrying about the things you cannot **control**. What you can control is how you **react** in such a situation. Trust in God to take care of the rest and focus on doing your work in the meantime. Things will become alright, and you shall reach your destination. Here are a few quotes to ponder when you need to inspire, motivate, and uplift yourself to follow your passion.

"Believe in your infinite potential. Your only limitations are those you set upon yourself."

-Roy T. Bennett

This is a beautiful quote that focuses on a very important aspect of the human mind. You are oftentimes reduced in potential by your own **limiting beliefs** and nothing else. Have **faith** in your talent and abilities to the fullest. Many a time we tend to underestimate ourselves more often than not. Give yourself the credit you deserve, and take pride in the same. Every time you think you **can't**, keep telling yourself that there is always a *way*. You only need to seek it, and you will find it.

"Just don't give up trying to do what you really want to do. Where there is love and inspiration, I don't think you can go wrong."

-Ella Fitzgerald

Here is a quote that emphasises the fact that when you have nothing but the *purest* of intentions and aspirations, things never actually go wrong when you're working toward your goals. When you truly *love* doing something, don't ever give up. Things may not always be great but the tough times also come to pass, and you will be able to see again. Giving up is an easy choice, but to keep striving regardless takes effort and a strong *mindset*. Train yourself to be *resilient* even during tough times and you'll become undefeatable. Your *dreams* are worth being chased and recognised, so do not ever give up on them, as you can most definitely do it.

"Don't be satisfied with stories, how things have gone with others. Unfold your own myth."

-Rumi

Just because someone else's story went awry does not mean that yours has to end the same way too. People have *different experiences* and may have various approaches and perspectives to how they see things. Don't let someone else's story affect the way you feel about yours. You are your own person and you are blessed with *infinite potential* to do anything you want. Be the maker of your own story. Regardless of how things go you'll live without regrets. Everyone has their own **unique** story to tell. Go ahead and start creating your own. Your story deserves to be written, and it is solely yours, and yours alone.

"I attribute my success to this: I never gave or took any excuse."

-Florence Nightingale

You will be faced with several obstacles on your path, but having **zero tolerance** for excuses will prove extremely useful. You only approach a stunt so long as you stop searching for **solutions**; it is when you stop you fail. As long as you keep trying there is no such thing as failure, so get up, keep working, keep getting better. Don't take failure as an option; it is part of the journey but not the ultimate goal. Your goal is the only option, and with this in mind, you will have better focus on what you want. Every time you come up with an excuse to stop, remind yourself of reasons to keep going. **Success** becomes inevitable; you become a force to behold, and leave the rest to God.

"I choose to make the rest of my life the best of my life."
-Louise Hay

Be **grateful** for everything you have at the moment, but if you find that you are not satisfied with the way things are as of now, or you have a feeling that things could be better, then work toward creating that life. It's never too late to start; no matter how old or young you are, you can always work toward a **better life**. I'm pretty sure that everyone has an image of what it is that they envision their lives to be, but sometimes life and responsibilities catch up to us, and we might forget what we had once wanted for ourselves. Take some **time** for yourself, rid yourself of all the distractions, and think, is this what you've always wanted? Is this the life you've always dreamt of? If yes, then that's great for you. If no, then you still have a chance to build the life you want. Start now, this very moment. Start little by little. Every **small step** you take will get you one step closer to your **dream life**.

"If you are working on something that you really care about, you don't have to be pushed. The vision pulls you."
                                                              -Steve Jobs

You know you're truly **passionate** about something when it never tires you out, and you don't have to force yourself to do it. The vision of it all is more than enough motivation. Doing the task **exhilarates** you, and you feel joyous and alive when you're doing that particular task. It's a feeling unlike anything else. It's like a **calling** from deep within your soul, a silent voice constantly guiding you toward that one thing. Your **purpose**, your vision; we often don't hear that little voice amidst our busy lives these days, and this is where a decent moment of quietness will do you a lot of good. If you want to find out what it is you're truly passionate about and focus on the things that bring you joy, meaning, and a sense of **contentment**, work toward it.

I sincerely hope that these quotes bring you light amidst dark, heavy, and tough times. Or even when you need a boost of energy, just give these a quick read and you should be good to go. Remember, the road to success is not a **straight line**. There are ups and downs, so even if you're going through a low this doesn't mean that all is lost. Have faith in God when things are uncertain and you find yourself getting anxious. It is all part of the **journey**; the journey is what makes success a beautiful thing and much more significant than the end goal itself. So keep going, don't worry about what will happen next, and focus on what you can do right now. The rest will be taken care of.

"Success means having the courage, the determination and the will to become the person you believe you were meant to be."

-George Sheehan

AI-generated picture

Vision Board: I collect inspirational and motivational quotes to encourage and stimulate me

When Words Fail but Passion and Action Say it All

"Be yourself. An original is always worth more than a copy."

-Suzy Kassem

Dear Reader,

Psalm 128:2 says, *"You will eat the fruit of your labor; blessings and prosperity will be yours"* and Proverbs 14:23 says, *"All hard work brings a profit, but mere talk leads only to poverty."* It's easy to speak a lot about what you want in life, but the real task lies in whether you take **action** toward achieving your goals. I'm pretty sure you've heard of the phrase *it's easier said than done*. The real task lies in taking that one step every day, without fail regardless of what happens, that gets you closer to your goals. **Hard work** and **persistence** always pay off and you will most definitely enjoy the fruit of your work. **Genuine effort** is always rewarded. Have strong faith and pave your path with determination. You will excel at what you do if you are authentic, hardworking, persistent, and consistent.

I may not always have the fancy words or extensive vocabulary to express myself, but I take it as a **strength** of mine as I show my dedication, diligence, leadership, and compassion in my personal life and career through **actions** rather than **words** without substance. I'm an **action-oriented** person and strongly believe that when your actions align with your goals and mindset, you become truly remarkable. I take great pride in the fact I was able to keep myself focused and dedicated to my goals and ambitions despite everything that I was faced with, and you too can do the same. Even if it's not a big step, taking one step at a time is more than enough, for in the end, it's the *smaller steps* that make it count. Actions are the proof of what you claim you are.

It was my ability to express myself through *action* that enabled me to sharpen my *skills* in my job and business. Keeping at it daily made a big difference in how well I performed. It's not just about working hard but doing it regularly. It was the *consistency* that boosted how good I got at what I did. I've learned that when you put in effort regularly, it makes a bigger *impact* than just trying hard once in a while. It's like the *snowball effect* – the more I keep at it, the better I get. I firmly believed that sticking to this routine would keep pushing me toward even more success in the future. Hence, I've committed myself to this path, knowing that it's the surefire way to achieve my goals and keep growing in my *career* and *business*. Pursuing my dreams nurtured me as an individual both mentally and physically. I grew not just in my profession but as an *individual* too.

This has also helped me *fine-tune* my *talent* in my career and business. No person is born excellent in any field; even if they are, it takes *consistent* practice and *effort* to maintain it. You can become a master in any field you wish to excel in if you put in consistent effort and dedicate time to it. *Practice* makes perfect. Keep *leveling* yourself up every day, even if it's simply by just a step, and focus on becoming the **best** at what you do. There is never knowing too much; knowledge is vast, and no matter how much you learn there is always more to it, so keep **learning**, keep yourself updated and efficient. In this way, we remain mentally healthy as learning keeps the mind and brain active and strong. You can call it **mental muscle**. You're building mental muscle and this will serve you well in the long run.

Remember to **stay true** to yourself and not try to be someone else. Being your **authentic**, truest self will change your life. You perform and **excel** when you are yourself. When we try to be someone else, we are forcing ourselves to put **effort** into someone that we are not. This effort doesn't align with who we are and our **true purpose**, hence doing us no good, so let go of all your fears and be yourself with **confidence**. You are your own **unique** person and you deserve to be seen and heard just as much as anyone else. Own your **strengths** and **weaknesses** both, and walk with pride. You are worthy of everything the world has to offer and by being yourself you are opening yourself up to the same.

When passion and action go hand in hand you reach your goals much *faster* and more **efficiently**, and frequently you will find yourself not even having to push yourself to work toward it as it becomes purely **effortless**. People say things like, *it's hard, you can never make it, it's tiring, it's impossible*, but in all honesty, once you've worked through the initial **friction** the process becomes easy. It's just like practicing any other skill; the more you do it, the easier it gets. ***Passion*** serves as the driving force, the fuel igniting your journey. It's that deep-rooted love for what you're chasing that keeps you going, making the process seem less of a chore. When you're passionate, work becomes play, and effort transforms into enthusiasm. It's not about forcing yourself but about being pulled by an unseen force propelling you forward.

Effortlessness doesn't mean absence of effort; it signifies ***alignment***. When passion and action converge, effort transforms into a seamless flow. It's not that the path is devoid of challenges, but your approach makes overcoming them a natural part of the ***journey***. In essence, it's a symphony – passion composing the melody, action providing the rhythm. And when both of them harmonize, the result is a masterpiece of achievement. So, amidst the myriad of doubts and impossibilities, remember, your dreams await, ready to be brought to reality through the unity of your passion and action.

Remember, there is a reason why you've always been ***passionate*** about that one thing. Do not ignore that voice within you that guides you toward your ***purpose***, or anything you'd like to call it. Even if the ***unknown*** seems scary, embrace the uncertainties and have faith that ***God*** will hold your hand and take you safely through your path. Train yourself and build ***resistance***. It is straightforward to give up and say that you can't do it, but your success lies in getting up after each fall and striving to ***better yourself***. It's okay to make ***mistakes*** on the way, but ***learn*** from them and next time you're faced with a similar situation, you know what to do.

Actions, more than mere words, resonate as your true self. They possess equal power, if not more, in validating your convictions. Meanwhile, *passion* is the driving force, breathing life into your beliefs. It's this fervor that shapes your actions, manifesting your innermost *values*. Actions act as imprints, narrating your story, and revealing your *sincerity*. When words falter, actions become unwavering proof, embodying your dedication and core principles, communicating volumes about your character and what you uphold. When genuine intentions prevail, actions often speak louder than words. Wishing my dear readers the very best on their journeys!

"If you can't fly, run; if you can't run, walk; if you can't walk, crawl; but by all means keep moving."

-Martin Luther King Jr

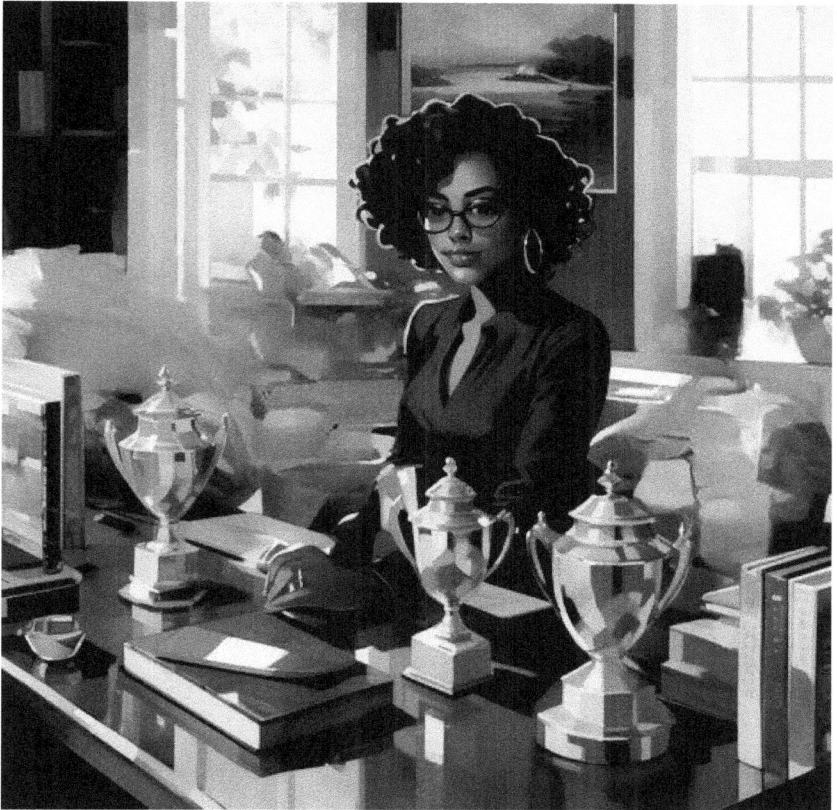
AI-generated picture

Awards and Rewards: evidence of my passion and action fueled by my faith

My thoughts…

For years I believed William Shakespeare's quote that "some are born great, some achieve greatness and some have greatness thrust upon them."

I saw myself in the category of achieving greatness someday, but now, in my boldness I positively challenge what Shakespeare said while I navigate life's journey, and I encourage my readers to ponder on my words:

"We're all born great, we can all achieve greatness, and we all have greatness bestowed upon us. We just have to discover our identity, our source, our purpose, our potential and destiny and then believe."

Remember, You're Valued!

Thought Provoking Questions

Some of us may find it challenging to dedicate protected time to explore what it is we value in life, our goals and much more.

As such, the following pages have been added to this book to nudge readers to write down their thoughts and take action. It's an encouraging way to enable you push beyond the boundaries of your comfort zone and start thinking outside the box if you haven't already been doing so.

It will start you on the path to discover who you are as a person and perhaps as a compassionate leader. **Who are you?**

It will enable you to start thinking about where you draw your strength from; that is, **where is the source of your strength?**

You'll be able to ask yourself the question of why you are in the job you're doing and think through your answers. **Why are you here?**

If you are in your dream job, then you can challenge yourself to explore your potential – **what can you do better in your job?**

Answering the above question will enable you figure out what your goal or destiny is. **Where are you going from here?**

Thought Provoking Questions

Who are you?

Thought Provoking Questions

Who are you?

Thought Provoking Questions

Who are you?

Thought Provoking Questions

Who are you?

Thought Provoking Questions

Where is the source of your strength?

Thought Provoking Questions

Where is the source of your strength?

Thought Provoking Questions

Where is the source of your strength?

Thought Provoking Questions

Where is the source of your strength?

Thought Provoking Questions

Why are you here (in your job, etc.)?

Thought Provoking Questions

Why are you here (in your job, etc.)?

Thought Provoking Questions

Why are you here (in your job, etc.)?

Thought Provoking Questions

Why are you here (in your job, etc.)?

Thought Provoking Questions

What can you do better in your job, etc.?

Thought Provoking Questions

What can you do better in your job, etc.?

Thought Provoking Questions

What can you do better in your job, etc.?

Thought Provoking Questions

What can you do better in your job, etc.?

Thought Provoking Questions

Where are you going from here?

Thought Provoking Questions

Where are you going from here?

Thought Provoking Questions

Where are you going from here?

Thought Provoking Questions

Where are you going from here?

www.ingramcontent.com/pod-product-compliance
Lightning Source LLC
Chambersburg PA
CBHW071457210326

41597CB00018B/2589